Author Details

Geraldine Taylor is Educational Consultant to
Penguin's birth to eight publishing team, and a
counsellor for students at Bristol University.

**She is a multi-award winning author and was BBC
Wildlife Writer of the Year in 2000.**

Contact Geraldine on: geraldine.taylor1@virgin.net

THE COFFEE THRUSH

and other bird stories

Geraldine Taylor

**Illustrations by
Dru Marland**

*Eyeon Books
Bristol
2009*

The Coffee Thrush
and other bird stories

Author: Geraldine Taylor
Published by: Eyeon Books
Design: Keith Taylor

illustrations: Dru Marland
Tel: 0117 973 3575
Mob: 07977 125 824

Email: Drusilla.marland@btopenworld.com

ISBN 978-0-9551823-1-0

Eyeon Books
28, Berkeley Road, Bristol, BS6 7PJ
0117-973-2787

eyeon.books@virgin.net

FOREWORD

Birds are the treasures of our universe, like sweet
violets, and loyalty. I have loved birds all my life
and lately, have found myself particularly involved
with thrushes.

Geraldine Taylor

Dedication

"It is impossible for us not to love whatever is lovely, and of all living things birds are made most beautiful."

"Life is not life without them."

W. H. Hudson 1893
Birds in a Village

The Coffee Thrush
and other bird stories

One of these mornings
You're going to rise up singing

November 08

Sunrise. Three dog walkers and I stand round
this ivy covered ash, listening to the commanding
phrases of a song thrush, in the way that people
once gathered around bushes containing
nightingales.

Early one morning in February, I was passing a
bush just as the song thrush in it started to sing.
The bird warmed up with a loud medley sung
from the base; then it rose up through the
branches, singing with thrilling sharpness.

I talk to the birds, ask them how they are doing,
encourage them along. Sometimes they react
with clucky exasperation or by jumping in the air,
but often they continue singing while I listen and
watch. They are not singing for me, of course,
though my heart finds this impossible to accept.

Also, as a therapist, I find myself trying to make a relationship with everything I see.

Little Sister

December

The sky is pink and starless: the earth holds its breath. I can see the sun rising through a silhouetted snowfall of catkins. The blackbird is the first to cry out, with a call that gets the great tits started, and then the robin, and now the wrens' *chinks* and the chaffinches' *pinks*. Birds swap trees and branches like a party game. I'm looking up as I walk, and one of my feet crashes into a partly frozen puddle.

Another frozen puddle on Clifton Down and two magpies strutting over it and pecking the watery edges. A pied wagtail scuttles after them like their little black and white sister.

Rides of trees are intense, magical places, and I loved the Elm Ride across the Downs, long replaced by beech trees: I'm looking at the purple sweet violets flowering under one of them. There are puffs of mist and long whistles of starlings: perhaps a ghost train is travelling down the beech ride.   Young ride, new legends.

Apparently, the name of the wagtail in Arabic means Father of Salutation. I've just learned this from one of WH Hudson's letters (March 1920).
A perfect description of the pied wagtails that often fly towards me in bleak, concrete places, seemingly intent on offering a greeting.

The Coffee Thrush

January 2009

New Year's Day 7.40 am: minus four C.
I may never have been this cold before; I expect to see the Northern Lights. A pair of bullfinches is calling, a sweet *psue*. Three male blackbirds cluck about at the bottom of shrub islands. Rooks sit in pairs on the frozen turf, touching beaks.

Here is a green woodpecker dropping, looking like an ashy catkin. Can the bird be getting enough ants from this hard ground? Do not feel up to examining the dropping to find out.

Oh, this is no weather for the littlest birds. Even so, a flock of long-tailed tits is somersaulting through the limes.

I make a point of mentioning to the mistle thrush that he is perched on exactly the same branch of the same lime tree opposite the café at the same time as he was yesterday. I know this because I am preparing to enter the café from the same direction and at the same time as I did yesterday.

Usually, while I am having a second coffee, this mistle thrush flies into the holly tree outside the window of the Downs cafe. Once (in a witnessed incident, and to general applause) the bird flew in

just as my coffee arrived: I tapped the saucer
with the spoon and down came the thrush …

Last year, winter thrushes (redwings) feasted on
the holly berries here, but now the mistle thrush
has appropriated the tree.   Other customers ask
the café manager about the bird in the holly tree,
What it is? Why is it always there? I have
prepared a card about the thrush for the manager
to show people who enquire.

*Long-tailed tits find it hard to keep warm in winter
when insect food is scarce. Population falls of 80%
have been recorded in severe weather. They need to
search for food during all the hours of daylight. At
night, they roost by huddling together, like wrens.*

The Fairyland Thrush

February

I rarely hear song thrushes and blackbirds singing
together. This morning, song thrushes sing while
blackbirds whisper in bushes. Sometimes they
come to the edge of the bush and trill down the
scale.

I walk between five song thrush territories on the
Downs, hear all five birds but see only two.

I'm learning each thrush by the phrases it selects,
so I can talk with it about its music. Some choose
bubbling phrases, some chuckle, others converse
with me more earnestly. Most thrush songs are
those of a performer at the peak of his powers –
carefully balanced, impeccably sung.

This song thrush in Fairyland Wood, however,
begins with long notes that dip into the minor key,
and then silence. At first, I didn't even recognise
the song as a thrush's until the lengthy silence
was followed by repeated phrases.

This uncertain music tears at my heart with
things I thought were past grieving.

The drumming of the great spotted woodpecker!
Am overjoyed, and play with the bird's name,
deciding to call it a *drumpecker*. Other
examples of this are a greenfinch which is a
wheezer, a nuthatch a *nutter* and a chaffinch a
chaffer. A starling is a *false teeth bird*, but this
would take some explaining.

The Observatory Robins

March

Blackbirds are addressing the nation: from
territory to territory, treetop to treetop; beacons of
song all over the country.

Last week, the Coffee Thrush was not on the
holly tree outside the café.   He was, in fact, seen
flying rapidly past it in pursuit of *another* mistle
thrush.   Today, however, the bird is in place
again.

I have received a message of thanks from café
customers for my card about the Coffee Thrush.

The Fairyland Thrush has developed his song, yet
even his bubbling phrases suddenly crack as
though the bird hasn't the heart for it. I watch him
singing at the top of an ash, wings held slightly
away from his body. Sometimes I feel so sad that
I hurry away from the bird's territory – but it
takes time to escape the song's far carrying.

I kneel to do up my shoelace beside the hedge
circling Observatory Hill. At this moment, a
robin flies up to the hedge top from the other side
and sings! I stay hidden and enjoy the piercing
music. The hill is full of robins this morning,
and the crystal air holds and prolongs their ruby
song: birds of a small paradise.

Much of my daily work is reconciling troubled
young people to living. Perhaps one day they'll
find strength in the singing of robins.

Marble

March

Birders rush to tell me, *there is another Whitey!*
Whitey was a white and black jackdaw I loved
since he (or she, hard to know with jackdaws) was

a fluffy, dappled fledgling. I called him
Dalmatian Jack, though the birders persisted with
Whitey. Dalmatian's white markings, alas, made
him a target for the Gorge peregrines.

Now there is another one, patterned in flight like a
marbled white butterfly. She huddles in the
brambles watching the other jackdaws, and the
wind ripples her feathers.

What will the birders name her?
Will the existing jackdaw community allow her to
join them?

Did a previous community push her out?
Will she find a mate (Dalmatian did)
Will she dodge the Gorge peregrines? (Dalmation
didn't)

The birders are calling her *Whitewhistle*. I have
named her *Marble*.

Marble wasn't there today.

Nor today. I ask everyone to look out for her.

Other birders have taken Marble to their hearts,
too, although they are now calling her *Lucas*. No
one has news of her, not even the other jackdaws.

The evening song of my garden blackbird is
thoughtful, and full of repetition. Sometimes I fall
asleep to this lullaby.

There is a difference between the sharp morning
song of blackbirds, and the mellow evening song.
Earlier ornithologists suggested that we are
hearing different birds – young males in the
morning, and older birds in the afternoon. Mine
is unquestionably the same bird.

David and Goliath

April

Two Observatory Robins weave through the
hawthorn and fleetingly, sit together gossiping.
There's another Observatory Robin singing, but I
can't see it. Eventually a dropping lands at my
feet and I look up to find the robin on a branch
immediately above my head.

Am I imagining sadness in the song of the
Fairyland Thrush? The silences between phrases,
and the down-turning calls still grieve me.
However, he now incorporates a great tit
imitation, and an ironic cackle.

Nesting birds are losing interest in me, except as
an annoyance. They make this clear in their
alarm calls. This wren protests passionately - I
must GO AWAY! She has THINGS TO DO.

I witnessed a David and Goliath demonstration of
bird alarm in Leigh Woods.

A hot air balloon was descending, its basket
brushing the treetops. Dozens of birds united
against the giant intruder, their oaths and war

cries audible above the hiss of the balloon
burner. Suddenly the balloon found the lift to
clear the trees and continue its journey. The birds
went quietly about the business of the woods: job
done.

The Fairyland Thrush is singing above rush hour traffic. His song now includes gravely chuckles. I wonder if, like blackbirds, he sings a more reflective song in the evening?

Kentish Blackbirds

April

This Observatory Robin is singing like a thrush: trills, great tit verses, and repetition. I guess that our first awareness of individual birdsong becomes our norm for that bird: all others seem variations.

 Many birds have regional tweaks in their songs – especially blackbirds, chaffinches and willow warblers. Kentish blackbirds often select a phrase similar to part of the third movement of Beethoven's violin concerto.

What a songster the Fairyland Thrush has become! His great tit imitation *teacher teacher* is *shouted* at the sky. Passers-by stand with me to listen and we laugh at his chuckling phrases.

The pretty verses of willow warblers sweeten my life. These little birds are in hawthorns and ash trees at all four corners of this tiny meadow - in the way that the English picnic at the edges of fields. Skylarks sing in the sky. I hope Heaven is as good as this.

Kentish Blackbirds are those west of the Medway. Blackbirds to the east of the Medway are Blackbirds of Kent. I wonder if the Beethoven phrase has spread to the east of the river.

The Birds in the Band

April

Time to be a woodlander: off to Leigh Woods.
It's raining, but the show must go on and birds
often sing their best songs in the rain.

Here are the Birds in the Band – the blackcap
fanfare at the wood entrance, nuthatches around
the bluebell glades, blackbirds slipping between
yews, a wren fussing at the tree roots of this
badger sett, the song thrush on the high rise ash,
drumpeckers in the shadows, and robins in sunny
patches. And a jay at Jay Corner, ranting about
the state of the woods.

*Thrushes, blackbirds, blackcaps and dunnocks
sing in the rain. A dawn chorus on a damp
morning is vigorous event.*

*I have heard that the nightingale also sings with
particular enthusiasm in light rain, but cannot
confirm this myself.*

No Sudden Movements

May 1

This may be the last entry in this book. I will be too ashamed to continue: I do not deserve the title of bird lover. This morning I flung open my window at five, to enjoy the first dawn chorus of May. Unfortunately, this was the very second that the blackbird nesting in the holly tree under my window was returning with food for his nestlings. He hovered in desperate uncertainty, then flung himself into the tree to his mate, with a hysterical scream. The female immediately shot out of the tree with him, over the rooftops and far away.

Will they come back? Will their nestlings starve? Will I hear their abandoned cheeping and then the terrible silence?

Blackbirds are the most conscientious of parents and have no sense of humour. I have already modified my behaviour so as not to disturb them. I eject cats and magpies. I change the water in the birdbath quietly. I do not sit out on my garden chairs. I do not weed near the holly. I have stopped my pet rabbit burrowing under the tree. I congratulate the blackbird on his singing. I know how privileged I am to provide a haven for birds. *They know I am on their side.*

But the rule is *no sudden movements*, even on the first of May.
Will I ever learn?

This morning, I visit my birds with a heavy heart. Neither the Fairyland Thrush, nor the Observatory Robins can lift my spirits. I thank them mechanically, and I brood on the fate of Marble.

Later: The blackbirds have returned, but the male has been giving me high-minded tilts of his beak all afternoon. However, I do think his scream and scarper on seeing me at the window this morning was a bit *much*.

Ballad in a Beech Wood

May

Unusual (see *February*). Deep in this beech wood, a song thrush is engaged in a ballad with a blackbird. Each bird sings when the other pauses: each waits a second before taking his turn as though making sure that the other has completed his verse.

This luminous green exists only in the leaves of the beech in spring. And above the beeches, look - the swifts are back!

The Bird of Perfect Summers

May

Meadow now, in Ashton Court Estate where the bird song is as thrilling as the morning: skylarks on scramble, rising up singing; goldfinches ringing like bells atop blossomy hawthorns; willow warblers in small corners, tiptoeing into song.

The willow warbler is the bird of perfect summers, now and long ago. Their dainty song

melts our hearts. Nature writers write lyrically about these little catkin coloured birds, and birdwatchers speak of them with great affection. I wish I could know willow warblers as individuals like the Coffee Thrush or the Observatory Robins.

I wonder, for example, if the length of their song varies between individuals: although I have reservations about turning up in the meadow with a stopwatch to time them. What is it like to hear willow warblers in the dawn chorus? Can they hover like sparrows and blue tits?

Sparrows and other small birds can hover like hummingbirds for short periods. I've seen a sparrow hover for over a minute to catch flies under a garage roof: once, I saw a robin attempt this, less successfully. Sometimes blackbirds hover for a second or two and this is usually the product of indecision. Blue tits include a hover in their fussy flying pattern – land on a branch, take off and hover; land on another, take off and hover, and so on. It's pretty to watch, especially around hazel bushes in the sunshine.

The Littlest Birds Sing the Prettiest Songs

June

I have overcome my reservations about turning up in the meadow with a stopwatch!

The shortest willow warbler song is 2.2 seconds, and the longest 5.4. I had imagined the song was longer, at least 8 seconds. And even singers of such tiny fragments can bring variation to their melodies. Willow warbler A is tentative and reflective; willow warbler B is confident, funny and his song has surprising carrying power: I can hear it over the din of the nearby rookery. Willow warbler C flits through the woods, singing quietly in response to willow warbler B, like an echo. There should be a willow warbler D as the birds are in all four corners, but this bird is so far silent.

I must study *how* these birds vary the length of their songs, where the extra notes and pauses are placed, and how much variety there is in the verses of an individual. Also how often these birds sing each minute, and how many times an hour.

I once spent an entire summer day in Kent investigating the songs of yellow hammers.

Some thoughts about humour and birds

I wonder if what we react to as funny in birdsong is the timing, pauses and surprise, in much the same way as we respond to comedians. For example, sad phrases followed by a long pause followed by gravely chuckles as in the case of the Fairyland Thrush. Or quiet reflective notes, followed by upbeat bright ones, as those of Willow Warbler B.

More thoughts, this time about birds and happiness

I wish I could use my feeling for birds more often in my work with distressed young people. Sadness and anxiety detach us from the energy of the wildlife world and I believe we need this outdoor energy to feel real, and hopeful. Sometimes a blue tit or jay comes close to my window at work, and my client's face lights up in delight, a feeling that their words haven't yet shown me.

Often, when we are unhappy or grieving, we long to change, but our heart reserves the right to remain the same. Fortunately, birds, wildlife, are always around us, as an alchemist or as a lifelong consolation. I lose awareness of my life in the goings-on of theirs.

Being so much with wildlife has shown me how comfortingly little I matter; yet how much I, *we* have: how much beauty, how much recovery and renewal. I'm thankful, and I try to live generously.

For myself, also, I cannot see a bird without grinning, and I find this particularly helpful on difficult mornings.

If anyone requests it, I will talk a little more about my work as a therapist and my thoughts about the value of bird watching, in future books of bird stories.

Chirrup

18th June

4.30 am: The male blackbird nesting in our holly tree is singing in a mellow, low-key way. I think the blackbird sings now (when most other birds are silent) to teach his second brood the blackbird songs. Birds' need to sing is instinctive but the actual song has to be learned. This surely accounts for other late singing birds – dunnocks, chaffinches, chiffchaffs, greenfinches and thrushes: the Fairyland Thrush continues to sing. I wonder if there is a difference between the songs of first and later broods?

6.40 am: One of the blackbird chicks has fallen from the nest into my vegetable frame. It is staying on its side and I see that its leg is deformed, probably from being squashed in the nest.

The little bird is golden brown and speckled, with a yellow gape; huge eyes, and a beak tilted in the same way as its father's. But it can't balance and it wobbles, and tips over on its beak. I can't put it back in the nest: it will fall out again.

2.15 pm: The baby is still in my vegetable frame. Its balance is better and it is chirping and looking around. We phone a vet who is kindly and tells us to bring the baby bird in, though there may be nothing they can do about the leg. We prepare a cardboard box for the bird.

But now the parents are feeding the baby vigorously and we decide to leave it to them and phone the vet again. They understand and say if we do bring it in, the RSPCA would probably pay the bill, as we had intended to do ourselves.

If only human care and money could solve this.

How will it survive the night? Cats?

19ᵗʰ June

The baby is alive; heart-beatingly, fluffily, beak-gapingly alive.

I call the father blackbird *Zigmund* (for the benefit of my weekly BBC Radio Bristol programme) and now I must stop waiting for this little bird to die, and give it a name. I have called her Chirrup*. The parent blackbirds are feeding her frequently, dividing their time between Chirrup and the young still in the nest.

Even if Chirrup does fly, what about her leg? How would she perch? Maybe a vet could help at that stage. Chirrup is getting stronger by the hour: she is preening and stretching her wings. Now Chirrup is trying to fly! She is making feathery launches out of the vegetable frame that end in somersaults, yet she knows the power in her wings.

One of the other nestlings has made a dramatic flight out of the nest! Now the parents have their attention fully stretched. This other nestling is

* He or she? Impossible to tell.

much larger than Chirrup. Chirrup must have been the runt of the nestlings.

Another night.

20th June

20th June

6.00 am: Chirrup is in the vegetable frame, straggly after a night of rain, and looking up at the holly tree she fell from. She is shuffling in and out of the vegetable frame using the hole my rabbit is digging under it to get at the radishes. She takes strength from her mother's food visits and after each visit, she tries to fly.

11.20 am: Chirrup has made her way out of the frame again and is sitting in the rabbit hole outside it. My rabbit is in the garden and making for her hole beside the frame. I am afraid she will frighten Chirrup, but find her sitting by the bird and trying to lick the side of its face. My rabbit is gentle, but territorial and this is already beyond what I had believed possible for these two creatures, so I am beginning to hope for a miracle for this little bird.

Chirrup now shuffles away from the frame and settles under a lily of the valley leaf.

2.30 pm: Oh no, no, sudden, terrible noise in garden. We rush out and a black cat is scrambling up the wall with Chirrup in its mouth. I have never heard parent blackbirds so angry, and now so anguished.

I know the odds against Chirrup's survival; don't tell me, I *know*. But if there was a wild creature I so wanted to beat the odds, it was this gutsy little broken blackbird.

Also from EYEON BOOKS

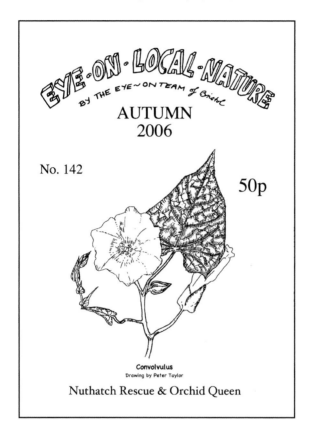

EYE·ON·LOCAL·NATURE
BY THE EYE~ON TEAM of Bristol

AUTUMN
2006

No. 142

50p

Convolvulus
Drawing by Peter Taylor

Nuthatch Rescue & Orchid Queen

Since 1982, from first cuckoo to last violet, EYE ON Magazine keeps you in touch with what the birds, plants, animals and trees are doing, via cowslips, tree creepers, butterflies, crab spiders, wood ants, badgers and peregrines.

By post, quarterly: £3.00 for 4 issues, by cheque or PO, payable to G. Taylor, 28 Berkeley Rd, Bristol BS6 7PJ

"A delightful newsletter" **The Times - 6 December 2008.**

Other Books by Geraldine Taylor

ECHO LANDS – and other true tales of the Avon Gorge Woods

An extraordinary account by award winning author Geraldine Taylor, recording her experiences of twenty-first century woodlanding: early morning wanderings in the woods each day before work, open to whatever wildlife – and human – dramas come her way.

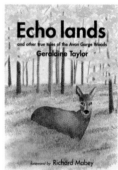

"Sparkling explorations" Richard Mabey, BBC Wildlife Magazine.

£4.50 Post free*

THE BRISTOL DOWNS – a natural history year

Geraldine Taylor's new book about the flora and fauna of the Downs. Each month, she gives two different walks with maps, and showcases the seasonal changes. With over 200 original drawings by Dru Marland to help identify the rich variety of plants, birds and other wildlife on the Downs. An ideal gift for all amateur naturalists and new wildlife watchers.

£6.50 Post free*

"Her own monthly diary with excellent notes." The Times - 6 December 2008.

* *To order, send cheque or PO payable to G. Taylor to: Eyeon Books: 28, Berkeley Road, Bristol BS6 7PJ*

Talks by Keith Taylor

1. Wildflowers of the Avon Gorge
2. The Cotswold Wildflower Show

Over 100 high quality colour slides in close-up of the rare, the beautiful and the bizarre plants that grow in Bristol, Somerset and Gloucestershire. Entertaining and informative. Keith's work has been featured in BBC Wildlife Magazine. He is a past president of Bristol Speakers.

To Book, phone: 0117 973 2787
or Email: eyeon.books@virgin.net

Pictures by Keith Taylor

Beautiful hand made pictures in frameless mounts, selected from Keith's best wildlife photographs. Make ideal presents. Freestanding if required. Selection of 12 flowers and butterflies. Size A5 approx. £2.50 each post paid.

For details, phone: 0117 973 2787
or Email: eyeon.books@virgin.net